Look at the Clou...

by Jay Dale

illustrated by Anna Hancock

"Look at the clouds," said the monkey.

"Look at the clouds," said the bird.

"Look at the clouds,"
said the spider.

"Look at the clouds," said the butterfly.

"Look at the clouds," said the ant.

"Look at the clouds,"
said the ladybird.

12

"Look at the clouds," said the caterpillar.

15

"Look at the clouds!"
said the frog.

16